Dreaded Thoughts

SAMUEL AGBONKPOLO

Published by: Polo RX, LLC

First published in 2023

Polo RX, LLC can bring authors to your live event. For more information or to book an event, contact Polo RX, LLC at polorxllc@gmail.com

ISBN-13: 979-8-9872976-0-5 (pbk)

ISBN-13: 979-8-9872976-1-2 (ebook)

Printed in the United States of America

Samuel Agbonkpolo
DREADED THOUGHTS

Dedicated to:

My angels on Earth I call family.

Contents

Dreaded Thoughts

BECOME SPOKEN WORDS

I. Genesis

It's been energy since energies been

It's been energy since the start, let the story begin

It's been energy in the dark, let there be light

It's been energy since "In the beginning"

In the beginning, it was dark

They saw less and feared more

Now, let them hear less and see more

While you stand fearless and be more

They can tell by your demeanor

That you live for something that means more

Sometimes you might come off as mean

Other times you might have to be mean or,

You could lose it all to someone less hungry

Some body less muddy,

No wonder they appear cleaner

Spending your energy attempting to make them believers,

Eager for the attention of those who oversee us, to see us

It was not too long ago when they originally oversea'd us

To take over the mind and have the body leave us

To plant all the seeds, while they over seed us

Watching the news will leave you praying to Jesus

Or wondering why, jeez us

Outnumbered physically, it takes a group to beat us

Hence why so much energy goes into division,

Together as a group they could never beat us

Our greatness can't be dimmed,

They will always see us

Darkest in the room, still we are the light,

From alpha to omega,

The energy will always be us.

II. Like This, Like That

I used to pray for times like this,

To write like this

Crazy how after all these years,

We still have to fight like this

"Lets give them Juneteenth as a holiday,

Yeah they might like this"

"Or post black lives matter on our page,

 Big and bright like this"

We've been done wrong for so long,

They can't make it right like this

Deliberately associate anything black with the negative,

Black-mail, black-ball, black-list, black-market

400 years later, black culture and bodies

Are still sustaining the market

From "property" to three-fifths a person,

To now, we remain the main target

If we stepped out of line, whips, chains, guns

Our skin, they would mark it

Now criminalized for whips, chains, guns,

The ink we put on our skin and how we mark it

The evolution of last place,

The cheese of the rat race

Many years at the bottom,

But it gets forgotten that black doesn't crack

That's why we walk this way and talk like that

Why we act like that and survive like this

Intended to break us, but now

Embedded pressure is why we shine like this

Twenty-twenty,

Never thought there would be a sight like this

Now I pray at times like this,

Because no longer will we remain the prey like that.

III. Sticks And Stones

Sticks and stones, may break my bones

But words, I have my way with words

Even when things don't go my way with words

Sometimes I spend all day with words

Thinking about what can I say

Wondering if you'll even allow me to say a word

Sometimes it's as simple as

Just say the word

You know what to say to make me laugh

And my anger words

You can either unload the clip

Or pull the trigger

With how you phrase your words

Or say less, do away with words

My actions have proven

I can hold my weight with words

Take time to wait and consider

Before you say a word

Be mindful of your mind state

Before you state a word

Words of affirmation is a form of love

Love is not a game to be played

So don't play with words

Sticks and stones may break my bones

But words, words can hurt me.

IV. Beautiful Girl

Beautiful girl how should I describe you,

Should I flaunt you to the world or try to hide you

I want you to know, I'm not trying to get up inside you

I'd rather chill, watch a movie and lay right beside you

Sometimes, I sit back and look at chu'

I'm not talking about sneezing,

But God sure blessed you

And he definitely had a reason

See its not only your face and body that's appealing

But that smile that you wear,

It makes me want to express the way I'm feeling

I just don't know how I should talk to you

Should I put on a front or keep it raw with you

Because I'm not from the hood of LA

The home of the Dodgers,

Im from a city that dresses like Mr. Rogers

I'm on my grown man tip,

I'm done acting like a toddler

Because you don't need a dude who acts like a kid,

But a man who can be a father

Beautiful girl I've decided for now,

It's best you remain nameless

I'm going to paint this picture of you to the world

But to the world, you will remain frameless

If I say your name,

The world will start to judge you

Women will now stalk your social media

To put themselves above you,

Men from all over will now flood your messages

Telling you they love you,

But if you fall for that line,

Then I might be thinking too much of you

I'm hoping you're the one

Who can separate the bull from the realness

That it's not the truth you ignore,

And listen to the ignorance

So, Beautiful girl

I'm going to keep you on the hush for a while

Be happy with a hug,

And the opportunity to make you smile.

V. Material World

A lot of things on my mind

Realizing i made a lot of excuses

A lot of things in my possession

But the truth is, most of these things

Currently feel useless

Currently, stressing myself out

Trying to figure out why did I even do this,

Was I a prisoner of the moment?

Am I even going to use this?

Things I stayed up all night

Saved and prayed for

Had in the cart for days

Way before the day they got paid for

Way before the day I even got paid for

Working all them days

I spent hours wasting away

Thinking, there's so many hours in a day

If I work this much, save that much

I can't wait to spend the money made today

Now wishing there was more hours in a day

Time I can't get back

Free time, I chose to waste in the moment

Instead of being present in real time,

Spending time in the moment

I let time pass by,

Like the present was a pastime

Now the only thing on my mind is,

I'm done with the excuses,

I choose to be present in every moment

Remember your future depends

On how you spent your past times

In the moment.

VI. Beast Mode

Staring in the mirror,

Looking at my own reflection

Remembering the goals and endeavors

I had success in

While trying to forget the trials and tribulations

That kept me up stressing

They say within every curse is a blessing

Vice versa, and I believe that

They say time is money

If so, then there's a lot of time that I need back

There was times my goals

Felt like they were being defended by a d-back

As soon as my intentions reached the air

They were broken up by a deflection

Or intercepted,

Going in the opposite direction

Feeling as though I relapsed

Imagine, aimlessly thinking

You could move forward without a plan,

Now looking at your own reflection,

You ended up back where you shouldn't be at

Those who you thought would stay down

Are the main ones providing the negative feedback,

They thought they were up

Because you were down

Well, don't pass on an opportunity

To take the lead back

Take those words they're serving

Make them eat that,

Move in silence, like a G

Go beast mode like the lead back

They'll still want to discuss your downfalls

But even after you fall down

Remain about that action

Say less, and let them see that

Leave them speechless and in disbelief,

Wondering "gee, did you see that?"

They say the best stories are make believe

You're in control of your own story

It's not your job to make them believe that.

VII. Who Do You Love

Who do you love

Really, who do you love?

For you, is it like the fairytales,

Where your mate was sent from above?

Or does it begin with the physical

First comes the sensual hugs

Then you play masseuse

Feelings come after sexual love

Activating hormones and senses

But after a few moans and seconds,

You come to your senses

Asking yourself, is this love?

Or your ego crying for attention

Whether it's the place that's entered

Or front and center

Once standing at attention

When you lead with your ego

You end up in a space

Not in line with your intentions

They say love hurts,

Do you feel the tension?

It's deeper than the physical bond

Imagine the strain,

Attempting to break a covalent connection.

VIII. Mission Impossible

Mission Impossible: Growing old while black

Imagine the power in knowing that

Coming into the world

Not even knowing you're all black

They tell you to get somewhere,

You must know your history

Understand what happened,

What took place,

Ask yourself, "Why did they do this to me?"

Sold then taught their old history

Narrated with every intention to sell his story

Doing their very best,

To associate any thing black with misery

Think about it, anything black, is misery

Discuss black history in schools

Like a spiteful chore

As if our history is a bedtime story,

A natural antihistamine

The same repetitive four stories

As if you're a child and won't remember

"They already tried to sell this to me!"

Tried to sell the black father as a problem,

The black mother as a problem

Black children, black families, black thought

Now the solution to any black problem

Has become the most unsolvable mystery

As if they're not the ones who introduced

Unnecessary variables with their US history

Mission impossible, growing old while black

Where the definition of "us" always misses me.

IX. Dream Works

The difference is,

Some think about doing it,

While you couldn't stop thinking about it,

Until it was done

Peep how the scheme works

First, you allow any stress to leave your mental

Let your passions cross those barriers

Heavily concentrated,

They diffuse into your temple

Inception can cause things to feel coincidental,

Instead of questioning if you belong here

Be enthused,

You ended up where you were meant to

Wake up walking to a new beat

Moving at a new tempo

Your own thoughts become instrumental

So in tune with your why

Hard work is now exciting

Working hard becomes more fun than mental

The dream is the beginning

The work ethic is what instills the fundamentals

What makes a dream?

What makes a dream is no matter how it starts

At the very end, everything worked

Attempting to put the pieces together,

Wondering how it all worked out

How did all these characters,

Make the scene work

How did what started in your head

Now become what you see work

Any sleeping being can dream

But not all are willing to make them work

By any means

Whether financially or by the book

The definition of success

In any language means work

Do everything in your power

With everything that you have

To make every thing work

The difference is,

While some go to sleep to see their dreams

You can't wait to wake up

And watch your dreams work.

X. How Many Of Us Have Them

What about your friends?

Well, what about them?

Do they ride or die with you

Even when it's not about them

When it's all about you,

But you don't want to do it without them

Or do they only show up

When it's all about them

What about your friends?

Well, what about them?

You call to have a conversation with them

But it becomes one about them

You start to think to yourself

Are you better with them

Or without them?

What about your friends?

Nah, what about you,

It's never been about them

Ask yourself are you here today because of you

Could you have done it solely

Or is there a part in your story

Where there is no you without them

Remember, two things can be true

You can prioritize you and still be about them.

XI. Hocus Pocus

When you put your thoughts into words,

It is both powerful and dangerous

A moment of anxiousness runs through your mind

"Do I sound foolish?"

"Does this make sense?"

"No longer are these thoughts

Mine, mine, mine, all mine!"

The thoughts that were once in your head,

Have been confined to a few lines

But do these words

Spell out your thoughts how you imagined it?

It's as though the pen becomes your magic stick,

Just a bunch of hocus pocus

But let's not lose focus,

The power in writing thoughts down

Is the very way we stay focused

Don't doubt your thought process, own it, feed it

Take note of your progress, bold your goals,

Then come back and re-read it

Of course protect your thoughts at all costs

But don't be afraid to write and speak them into existence

Allow your eyes to see, allow your ears to listen

What good is a train of thought with no eye witness

It will get lost, it will be as though the train never existed.

XII. Tales From The Hood

Imagine, year after year, day after day, asking

The thieves of your freedom, for freedom

Even after years of them telling your people

They already freed them

Enslaved and beaten,

Books, they weren't allowed to read them

Created generational wealth off their backs for the free

Stole resources, destroyed lineages,

Relied on their labor to feed them

For centuries, literally four centuries

Now, so divided you continue to believe

You need them to be in control,

From slave patrol to neighborhood watch

Who thought they would be so literal

Turning black murders into sitcoms

Recall the critically acclaimed episode

Of a child in a hood

Being watched by a neighbor in his own hood

Grabbing snacks, talking to a young girl

Thinking about how his bag of candy

Is going to taste so good

She's thinking he's happy

Because her phone voice sounds so good

Meanwhile, he's being labeled

A hoodlum up to no good

A "hood" killed by a neighbor

While the neighborhood watched

The elements of a successful sitcom

We used to resort to any means necessary for justice

Revolts, boycotts, protests,

Sit-ins would be the only time we sit calm

Powerful together, this was quickly realized

Now they resort to any means necessary for us to sit calm

And for our response to be "Oh, just this"

The same formula, mislead, separate, manipulate

Black bodies still being killed for entertainment

Repeatedly left lifeless in the streets

Only to see no charges upheld after the arraignment

Ask yourself, how can you watch this and sit calm

How much more trauma must occur

Before you can no longer contain it.

XIII. One, Two Step

Five, six, seven, eight

One thing about life

You can't skip steps

And don't confuse missteps,

With missed steps

Some things you still don't know

And won't understand until you face it

You wouldn't be surprised you tripped up

If you tried to take steps in a shoe

Before you laced it

It's not a race with anyone

But your own expectations

You're the one,

Who dictates what the pace is

Your moves must align with your goals

Missteps happen when the two

Are headed in two different places

Erase from your routine

Time that is wasted

Be intentional with your time

And end up surprised

By the milestones that replaced it

It's not about getting there first

But taking the first step

Which leads to the second,

The third, the fourth

It feels like a grand slam

Once you've covered all the bases

One thing about life

You can't skip steps

You can't truly advance

Without covering all the basics.

XIV. Calculus

I know my calculus,

It says you plus me equals us,

But does it take into account the exes

In the prequel us

How the past can manifest into the sequel

How unaddressed trauma can be lethal

To us too,

How it can cause a minor issue to blow up

And now not only affect us two

How it can make you unrecognizable to self

Now the relationship looks like Us 2

It's like we're speaking two different languages

Both confused on how what used to feel so safe

Now became so dangerous

You say you don't feel important,

You're not protected,

Blind-sighted,

Don't even know what to say to this

Thinking about how strange this is

Distracted by the variables

Instead of considering how each other

Perceived the things each did

Remember this is calculus,

The way to solve the problem

Is to not prioritize oneself

But to always think as us

If you plus me equals us

Attaching negativity to your name

Will never be the best thing for us.

XV. In The Heat Of The Night

Imagine having peace of mind

Without relying on this piece of mine

Imagine walking down a street without a piece

On a peaceful night,

Dreaming about getting some sleep tonight

Only to be approached in the heat of the night

By the boys that carry that heat in the night

One wrong word,

They're reading you your speaking rights

One wrong move,

Warm bodies turn cold in the heat of the night

All you wanted to do was make it home,

Rest in peace tonight

Leaving the resting piece, the Wesson piece

By where you sleep at night

Instead "get on your knees, hands up"

No justice, no piece

It has a different meaning tonight

In the streets is where you lay,

Rest in peace

Lord, all I ask, let me come home

In one piece, after a peaceful night.

XVI. Most Wanted

Picture perfect

How do you paint a perfect picture

When society is ready to frame you

For eating skittles or stealing swishers

They want to reference you as a thug

A menace, a hoodlum,

Rather than a child, young man or mister

The wrong move, you'll be put out of your misery

Then they'll call it a mystery

Unsure why things escalated

Say you posed a threat to their life

To justify why they fired shots

Until their trigger fingers started blistering

Now they're the only ones left

To paint the story we're picturing

Perfect scenario for them,

They did everything right,

Including reach for their gun

Even after you followed orders

Keeping your hands in plain sight

"Officer may I ask why you stopped me?"

Instead of deescalating the scenario

They request for backup, "Copy"

They insist you're resisting

Now it's the floor you're kissing

Twisting and turning to catch a breath

"Stop resisting!"

Never considering the breaths you're missing

Few moments later, BANG!

Story over,

But it feels like the end is missing.

XVII. '22 Bonnie & Clyde

Let's touch a mil together

While we eat a few meals together

Chit chat, small talk, then get to the real together

I like that our dreams become real together

I like when our skin touches

And how they feel together

It kind of seems like we have things so real together

The Bonnie to my Clyde

Though we don't rob, steal, or kill together

If we had to, we would do the drill together

We enjoy making moves

But prefer to remain still together

Live for the inside jokes and random quirks,

We hold near and dear together

Crazy how everything seems so right

As long as we're together,

Though the world is a big place dear,

We're still a big deal together

Husband and wife, we made a deal together

King and queen, the real deal together

Forever a chess game, last time that I checked

If my mate is ok, then I am to until forever

You are my real forever

Every day, every hour, every moment

You have my heart signed and sealed forever

Never apart, together

I can listen to your heart forever.

XVIII. Who Shot Ya

Shots, shots, shots,

Rarely given a shot, but shot often

Imagine the trauma

Associated with the word... shot!

When you heard shots often

How anytime you're given a shot,

It's said to be because

There was no other option,

"We thought we saw a weapon,

There was no other option"

"You're only good at sports,

There was no other option"

"Affirmative action, we had to make the hire

There was no other option"

So understand the hesitation

When getting shot is the only option

Told we should be the first in line,

We're at the highest risk

Of ending up in a coffin from coughing

But never been the first in line,

Though we're at the highest risk

Of ending up in a coffin from walking

You see the game is still being played,

Though the approach has softened

They create a problem,

Determine the best financial option,

Then squeeze middle men,

Into thinking they understand

Their financial options

Meanwhile, those at the bottom

Who don't have money to buy in

Can only hope to hold on to what's at the bottom

So is there really a choice

When presented with a singular option?

History repeating itself,

It appears to be a cycle we're lost in

Never the priority,

Until it's their money it's costing

Shots, shots, shots,

Rarely given a shot, but shot often

Closed captioning from the opposition

Will always present as though

There was no other option.

XIX. Murder Was The Case

Murder was the case that they gave me

Born guilty, a skin color unworthy of forgiveness

Convinced only help from above could save me

That only a colorless man out of this world,

Could forgive this, how did we miss this?

Continuing to put faith of getting home safely

Into the hands of the very people that hate me

Either killed by twelve or convicted by twelve

No room for reasonable doubt

Labeled a menace to society,

Judged by the very people that enslaved me

Now, all to do is dream about going home

On the way to the big house

Another method to keep a black family

Without a black man in the house

Then comes the case of Kyle Rittenhouse

Who decided to not sit in his house

But cross state lines to protect the streets

With a fully loaded assault rifle

To force rioters to get in the house

Articulated his intentions so well that night

Before and after the murders but on the stand,

He can't seem to get the words out

From within his mouth

The verdict, not guilty

By reason of self-defense,

Even after showing premeditation,

How does this make sense?

From the trial of Rittenhouse,

To the young man slain for being accused

Of breaking in the house

The murder of Ahmaud Arbery

Treated as though

He was committing an armed robbery

Something as simple as going for a jog

In broad daylight,

Can be the last image you saw of me

Are you kidding me,

It's really starting to bother me

It's evident they will do anything to get rid of me

From body blows, physically whipping me

Stripped of clothes, left wearing welts

Used to be a constant reminder of the hits to me

But once found to be built different,

The focus shifted to headshots,

Mentally stripping me,

Stripped of culture, stripped of history

Stripped from everybody directly related to me

Now it's hard to tell who's hitting me

Whether charged or in a casket

The case is closed, guilty of being a threat

After they intentionally endangered my safety

Any justification to keep us in a box

One step out of line,

It's back to the cage that encased me

Once kings, chiefs and your majesties

Rulers of our own world like Travis

And now our whole word is buried in travesties

Taught to believe this is the land of the free,

A place of liberty, when in reality

Murder is either the case

Or the result that's given to me.

XX. I Do

It's not about putting those words together

But about bringing two worlds together

Through the highs the lows,

The anything goes,

The bright days, dark times

The stormy weather

Two words, I do

No one can do us better

I can write you a five page letter

Of everything for you, that I can do

Similar to those that require a fan to sleep

I'll bring you peace, I will fan you

In a healthy pure way, never Stan you

Though I'm your biggest fan

You're my one and only

A respectable man would never Onlyfan you

I vow to love you until forever

Even through the moments

When it feels I can do anything but stand you

I remember this is a team sport

When you win I gain the upper hand too

Our lives are forever tethered

If pain were to strike your knees

I wouldn't be able to stand too

I want to thank you,

For allowing me to be the one

Who dropped to a knee,

Heart beating, I couldn't stand

Asked for your hand

And you trusted me to be the one

You extended your hand to.

XXI. Baby Don't Cry

Baby don't cry,

Can't wait until you're able

To keep your head up

Because the way it's currently set up

It feels like it can be fatal

When I attempt to lift your head up

When I attempt to change your diaper

When I attempt to change your get up

I catch myself admiring your legs moving

It's as if you really want to get up

And if I had to bet my money

I'd say you could honestly probably get up

When I see you, I see the whole world

Like anything is possible,

I'll do anything to give you a leg up

Baby don't cry, but if you do,

I'll be there to hold your head up

I pray you never want for anything

And for everything you need

I'll be able to set up

I pray you never experience the ugly truths

And become fed up

Because the world you were born into

Will keep their knees on your neck,

And never let up

Will enter your house unannounced

Light your bed up

Then before any casualties are pronounced

Loved ones will be blamed for their mess up

Baby don't cry,

No matter how they attempt to knock you down

From day one, I never picked my bet up

Remember, I will always believe in you

I know that you will get up.

XXII. Moral Of The Story

Imagine not putting in the work

And expecting the outcome to work out for you,

Now you're left wondering how come

Agreeing with everyone that doubted you

Stuck in the middle like Malcolm

Now the worries of those on the outside

Are the only thoughts surrounding you

Staring down from the mountain of excuses

You decided to build your house on

Failed dreams are now a topic of resentment

Another lost battle,

Another way to avoid accountability

Another way to place the blame of failure

On the side with your spouse on

Moral of the story,

Don't let your dreams die

Don't let others closed minds

Be the primary resource

Of where you gain doubt from

Keep your eyes open for those

Who hop on board after the victory

They didn't see how the setbacks

Are where you learned how to bounce from

Allow your mind to believe in your capabilities

Allow the words to come out of your mouth

Breathe air into your desired outcomes

Variables are a part of the equation

Your story wouldn't add up without some.

XXIII. The Ride

The thing about waves,

Through the highs and lows,

They keep flowing

The thing about waves,

No matter how many times they crash

They don't stop, they keep going

The thing about waves

No matter what's placed in front

They keep showing

Obstacles become obsolete

Opposition is forced to adjust position

The world left at its feet

The thing about waves

Through the turbulence

They continue to travel at a high speed

The thing about waves

They never stay down

They always rise to compete

The thing about waves

They rise after every downfall

They don't rest in defeat

The score is never tied

They pull through every tide with energy

From highs to lows, ups to downs

Keep going forward,

Keep showing up,

Don't stop until the ride is complete.

LIKE THIS BOOK?
Consider sharing it with others!

- Share or mention the book on your social media platforms. Use the hashtag **#DreadedThoughtsBSW**
- Write a book review on a retailer website.
- Recommend this book to your friends, family, book club, or class.
- Follow Samuel on social media and tell him what you like about this book. **(Instagram: ThePharmAnimal)**

www.ingramcontent.com/pod-product-compliance
Lightning Source LLC
Chambersburg PA
CBHW021426090426
42742CB00009B/1279